ESSAYS IN INTERNATIONAL FINANCE

No. 183, June 1991

HIGH INFLATION AND THE NOMINAL ANCHORS OF AN OPEN ECONOMY

MICHAEL BRUNO

INTERNATIONAL FINANCE SECTION

DEPARTMENT OF ECONOMICS
PRINCETON UNIVERSITY
PRINCETON, NEW JERSEY

INTERNATIONAL FINANCE SECTION
EDITORIAL STAFF

Peter B. Kenen, *Director*
Margaret B. Riccardi, *Editor*
Lillian Spais, *Editorial Aide*
Lalitha H. Chandra, *Subscriptions and Orders*

Library of Congress Cataloging-in-Publication Data

Bruno, Michael.
High inflation and the nominal anchors of an open economy / Michael Bruno.
p. cm.—(Essays in international finance, ISSN 0071-142X ; no. 183)
Includes bibliographical references.
ISBN 0-88165-090-0 (pbk.) : $6.50
1. Inflation (Finance)—Econometric models. 2. Economic stabilization—Econometric
models. 3. International finance—Econometric models. Title. II. Series.
HG136.P7 no. 183
[HG229]
332'.042 s—dc20   91-23185
[332.4'1   CIP

Printed in the United States of America by Princeton University Press at Princeton, New Jersey

International Standard Serial Number: 0071-142X
International Standard Book Number: 0-88165-090-0
Library of Congress Catalog Card Number: 91-23185

CONTENTS

LIST OF TABLES

LIST OF FIGURES

HIGH INFLATION AND THE NOMINAL ANCHORS
OF AN OPEN ECONOMY

1 Introduction: Between Garden-Variety and Hyperinflation

It gives me great pleasure to commemorate the distinguished economist Frank D. Graham by speaking on a subject that lies close to one of his major contributions, his pioneering study (1930) on hyperinflation in Germany from 1920 to 1923. Much of my talk will relate to high chronic inflation and its stabilization, a somewhat different, albeit extreme, inflationary process that, although not known in Graham's days, would, I am sure, have drawn his interest.

Graham begins his book by referring to a remark of Cliffe-Leslie that the greatest scientific progress in social matters is made when economic disorders raise vexing questions as to their causes. He continues by saying:

> In the study of social phenomena, disorder is, it is true, the sole substitute for a controlled experiment in the natural sciences. But it sometimes happens that, in the midst of disorder, events move so rapidly that we are not able properly to absorb them; disorder may be excessive even to the most detached of scientists. The course of inflation in Germany in the first post-war quinquennium had so much of this character that it has seemed to many to be incapable of throwing any light upon monetary problems. This most striking of monetary experiences has in consequence evoked a minimum of scientific curiosity (1930, p. vii).

There follows a footnote that substantiates this last sentence from the vantage point of the 1920s. It refers to a book titled *Foreign Banking Systems* (Willis and Beckhart, 1929), which declares, with reference to Germany, that "it would be useless to try to connect the development of the German currency from 1919 to 1923 with any theories of

This paper is based on notes initially prepared for the Frank D. Graham Memorial Lecture given at Princeton University in March 1989. A draft of the paper was subsequently read at a workshop in honor of Don Patinkin, held in Jerusalem in May 1990. I am grateful to Rudiger Dornbusch for a very useful discussion of the paper at that workshop. Research for this paper was partly conducted during brief stays at the National Bureau of Economic Research, with the support of the National Science Foundation, for which thanks go to both institutions.

1

money. . ." (p. 632).

This statement sounds even stranger in hindsight than it did to Graham, for the German hyperinflation has become one of the most researched episodes in monetary history and theory. Frank Graham was undoubtedly a pioneer in this matter.

Two topics in Graham's study are relevant in our present context, even though the dynamic process to be discussed will be a different one. One has to do with the circular chase between prices, money, and the exchange rate. Graham was concerned with the question of causality in this regard, and, although econometric techniques were not known at the time, he tried in his own way to trace leads and lags in the data. The second issue pertains to the costs and benefits of extreme inflation, and we shall turn to this below. Graham maintained the surprising view that inflation benefited Germany because it helped erode the real value of the required reparation payments. The motivation for high chronic inflation is somewhat different, but the basic notion that one has to look at the benefits (to the government) of inflation as well as its social costs will still apply.

Although the German hyperinflation displayed very extreme dimensions (at its height in October 1923, prices increased by almost 30,000 percent), it was not the only case in its category. Cagan's (1956) definition of hyperinflation (monthly rates over and above 50 percent, a five-digit annual inflation of more than 13,000 percent) covers several other European episodes in the 1920s (see Table 1 and Figure 1) and also in

TABLE 1

HYPERINFLATIONS, 1920-1924

(monthly percentages and numbers of months and years)

Country	Average Monthly Percentage Rate	Peak Monthly Percentage Rate (Date)	Number of Months with Inflation > 50% (> 25%)	Number of Years with Inflation > 100%
Austria	17	129 (8/22)	4 (10)	3
Germany	949	29,525 (10/23)	11 (20)	4
Hungary	17	98 (7/23)	5 (9)	3
Poland	33	275 (10/23)	9 (16)	3

SOURCES: Cagan, 1956, and Sargent, 1982.

2

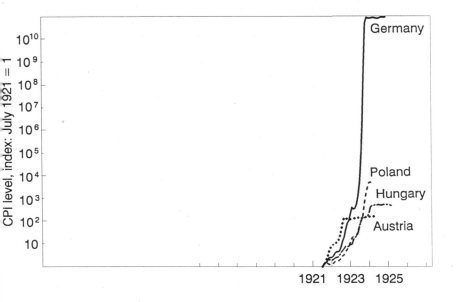

FIGURE 1

FOUR HYPERINFLATIONS OF THE 1920s

the 1940s (see Yeager, 1981). Hyperinflations of similar magnitude occurred again in very recent history—in Bolivia (1983-85), in Argentina and Brazil (after their respective 1985-86 stabilization programs collapsed), and also in Yugoslavia and Poland (1989) (see Table 2 and Figure 2). The common characteristic of all these episodes is their relatively short and highly explosive nature. Even if we define the range of the process to include sustained monthly inflation rates above 25 percent (more than an annual four-digit rate of 1,455 percent), the German hyperinflation lasted only twenty months, and the episodes of the 1920s in Poland, Austria, and Hungary lasted only between nine and sixteen months (Table 1). The length of the process was similar in Bolivia as well as in Argentina and Brazil, at least until the beginning of 1990 (Table 2).

The relatively short duration of the hyperinflation phenomenon is closely related to its highly unstable, dynamically explosive nature. It represents in most cases a virtual collapse of the monetary system, which can only be cured by a sharp fiscal and monetary reform. It is important to bear these facts in mind when considering high chronic

3

TABLE 2

HIGH INFLATION, HYPERINFLATION, AND STABILIZATION, 1970-1989
(monthly percentages and numbers of months and years)

Country (Year of Major Stabilization Program)	Average Monthly Rate [a] 1970-79	1980-85	1986-90	Peak Monthly Rate (Date)	Months with Rate > 50% (> 25%)	Years with Annual Rate > 100% 1970-79	1980-89
Chile (1975)	7.6	1.7	1.4	88 (10/73)	1 (1)	4	0
Bolivia (1985)	1.4	18.5	2.1	182 (2/85)	9 (16)	0	5
Argentina (1985)	6.8	11.9	19.0	197 (7/89)	3 (16)	5	10
Brazil (1986)	2.4	7.9	19.7	73 (1/90)	3 (16)	0	8
Israel (1985)	2.6	9.1	1.4	28 (7/85)	0 (1)	0	6
Mexico (1988)	1.2	3.9	4.8 [b]	15 (1/88)	0 (0)	0	3
Turkey (1980)	1.9	3.3	3.8	21 (2/80)	0 (0)	0	1
Yugoslavia (1990)	1.4	3.4	14.5	60 (12/89)	3 (7)	0	3
Poland [c] (1990)	0.3	9.6	8.6	77 (1/90)	2 (5)	0	2

SOURCE: International Monetary Fund, International Financial Statistics.

[a] Monthly averages refer to periods from January of the first year to December of the last year, except for 1990, for which most data reach only to January-February 1990.

[b] From April 1988 to April 1990, the average monthly rate was 1.7 percent.

[c] Based on annual data up to 1987 and monthly data for 1988 through 1990.

inflation, a relatively extreme but somewhat different inflationary process to which the cumulative experience of the 1970s and 1980s has drawn our attention. High chronic inflation is a much more prolonged and stable process that can last up to five or even eight years and can show monthly rates of inflation of between 5 and 25 percent, or annual rates in three digits. Table 2 shows data for Chile before 1979, for Argentina, Brazil, and Israel before 1985, and for Mexico before 1988. Although the origin of high chronic inflation, like hyperinflation, lies in the existence of a large public-sector deficit, the quasi stability of the dynamic process comes from an inherent inertia strongly linked with a high degree of indexation or accommodation of the key nominal magnitudes (wages, the exchange rate, and the monetary aggregates) to the

FIGURE 2

MAJOR INFLATIONS OF THE 1970s AND 1980s

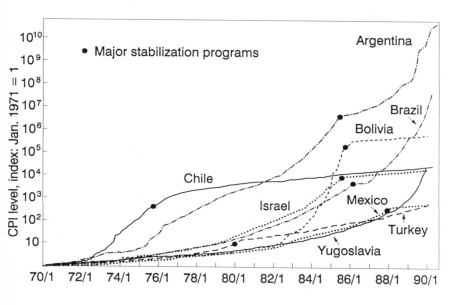

SOURCE: International Monetary Fund, International Monetary Statistics. The eight-country sample is analyzed in terms of recent experience in Bruno et al., 1991.

lagged movements of the price level. An inflation-prone system attempts to protect itself from the evils of inflation in this way, thus giving it a longer lease on life and delaying its more fundamental cure.

Moderate versions of chronic inflation having some of the same characteristics of indexation or monetary accommodation were already apparent in Latin America in the 1950s (see Pazos, 1972). As long as inflation stayed below a monthly rate of 5 to 6 percent, however (roughly corresponding to an annual rate of no more than two digits), its cure could be gradual, as in the case of the garden-variety, more conventional type of inflation. It was the large external shocks of the 1970s and 1980s, the oil shocks and debt crises, that brought about the new species of galloping, yet for a time quasi-stable, rate of inflation in the three-digit annual range. A gradual cure for this sort of inflation is unlikely to be feasible, yet the effects of shock therapy tend to be more complicated than for a hyperinflation because a persistent inflation memory has to be broken in addition to instituting the sharp fiscal reform. If the high inflation process is not terminated in time or if its stabilization attempt fails, however, it is most likely to lead eventually to a "classic" hyperinflation, as the recent experience of Argentina and Brazil illustrates.[1]

The various types or stages of inflation outlined here—roughly corresponding to the number of digits of annual inflation—can, in fact, be sequenced by the existence or absence of some key institutional or behavioral attributes. Failure to stabilize a stage I garden-variety inflation plus systematic indexing (and/or monetary accommodation) may lead to chronic inflation (stage II). In the presence of large price shocks, this may in turn lead to high chronic inflation (stage III). Failure to stabilize the latter will eventually move the system into hyperinflation (stage IV). Countries can, of course, move directly from stage I (or II) to stage IV without going through stage III at all. This has been true for most classic hyperinflations and is most probably also true for the most recent hyperinflations of Eastern Europe, in Yugoslavia and Poland, for example, where liberalization of a repressed price system could lead to hyperinflation almost at once.

The reason for focusing theoretical and policy-oriented interest on high chronic inflation is that it is a case in which, the system having lost its "nominal anchor," the dynamic nominal process may live a life of its own, almost independent of the size of the real budget deficit (the "real anchor"). This sort of "disorder" can be well grounded in the fundamentals of the neoclassical monetary system; any student of Patinkin's *Money, Interest and Prices* (1965) will have been taught that, when you double the quantity of money and double all nominal prices, the real system will stay invariant (chap. 3). This statement is, of course, nothing but an expression of the basic homogeneity postulate of the neoclassical model underlying the absence of money illusion, the neutrality of money as well as the so-called nominal-real dichotomy. Was this particular "nominal-doubling" experiment destined to remain only a mental exercise? As it happened, an almost ideal laboratory demonstration offered itself in Patinkin's own country twenty years later.

In 1981, it occurred to me while observing the inflationary process in Israel that we might be in the midst of an actual expression of Patinkin's experiment. For two years, Israel had been running a more or less stable

---

[1] For a study of recent high-inflation experience, stabilization, and its aftermath in the eight countries of Figure 2, see Bruno et al. (1991).

6

inflation rate of 130 percent per annum (7 percent per month)[2]—up from an annual 6 to 7 percent in the 1950s and 1960s and from accelerating two-digit inflations throughout the 1970s. By 1981, an annual nominal-doubling process was going on, seemingly divorced from the real economy and almost with a life of its own, although it was originally rooted in the real system and eventually nearly ruined it. All nominal variables—prices, wages, nominal assets, and the exchange rate—were moving in a quasi-steady state. Nominal or real shocks could change this steady-state inflation rate (and indeed they did), yet the same real system, including a persistent, reasonably stable, government deficit of approximately 15 percent of GNP, was consistent with several rates of inflation. A similar phenomenon was observed at the time in Brazil, where the inflation profile before 1985 was almost identical to Israel's, as well as in Argentina and, more recently, in Mexico and a number of other countries in which the nominal anchor has also been "lost" (see Figure 2).

It is important to stress that this phenomenon is relatively new. It is different from the much studied short and explosive hyperinflation process in being much more stable and therefore sustainable for a longer period. It also differs from the garden-variety inflations in exhibiting relatively small changes in relative compared to nominal prices. One manifestation of this property is the virtual disappearance of short-term Phillips curve tradeoffs.

This phenomenon could not persist for any length of time were it not for the inherent capability of exhibiting a nominal-real dichotomy. At an inflation rate of 7 percent a month, for example, a nominal-wage inflation of less than 6 percent a month would imply a cumulative real-wage drop of over 12 percent a year. This would obviously and eventually be resisted by wage earners, and a corrective formal or informal improved indexation mechanism would set in. Corrective measures would similarly prevent the real erosion of the money stock, which would eventually be accommodated even by a moderately independent central bank. The same applies to the erosion of the real exchange rate, the repercussions of which on the loss of foreign-exchange reserves would soon be felt, in the absence of a crawling devaluation, at a rate more or less equal to the inflation rate. In other words, once inflation reaches a high rate, institutional and policy mechanisms must set in

---

[2] The 7-percent monthly rate actually lasted four years, until 1983, when there was a large jump. This pattern shows in Figure 2 as a "flat" between 1979 and 1983 and as a kink in 1983.

7

that perpetuate inertia and quasi stability, unless a short-lived explosive or implosive situation quickly develops.

Given the empirical existence of a high-inflation process, we might ask two important sets of questions. The first is in the area of positive economics. Is a high inflation rate itself a random walk or can it be determined as an equilibrium solution to some rational (real) process? If such an equilibrium exists, is it unique (usually not) and what are its (or their) stability properties? Considerable work has been done in this area in recent years, based on a seigniorage deficit-finance framework (see Liviatan, 1983; Sargent and Wallace, 1987; Bruno and Fischer, 1990), but it is as yet incomplete. We shall here extend the existing discussion somewhat and motivate the existence of high inflation and its relative stability as the outcome of suboptimization by a "soft" government.

An obvious second set of normative policy questions follows. An inflationary process of the kind mentioned must have its roots in a fundamental disequilibrium of the real economy, invariably a sustained government and/or current-account deficit. Correction of the deficit, however, is in itself no guarantee that the inflationary process will not persist by force of inertia, sluggish expectations, or lack of credibility. Nothing in the dichotomous system makes such an outcome inconsistent with the real fundamentals unless the institutional arrangements perpetuating the dynamic nominal process are also broken. The very nature of the process described would suggest that there is room for a coordinated "shock" program that will simultaneously shift all the nominal components of the system from high inflation to a new zero-level, or relatively low-level, equilibrium to avoid sharp and destabilizing changes in relative prices. This is the conceptual basis for the so-called "heterodox" stabilization program. What, then, are the main nominal anchor (or several anchors) and set of rules on which the new equilibrium must be based? Could the choice of anchors change with the stage of disinflation?

Section 2 takes up a simple open-economy extension of the basic macroeconomic model and considers alternative anchors of the price *level*. Section 3 looks at the case of steady-state inflations and the nature of alternative equilibria. The choice of nominal anchors in the context of *rate* stabilization is taken up in Section 4, which discusses the pros and cons of using the exchange rate rather than a monetary aggregate as the key stabilizer, asks how that choice is related to wage-stabilization policy, and inquires whether a case can be made for the choice of more than one anchor even though the system could then be

8

overdetermined. The essay concludes with some empirical observations based on recent policy experience.

2 The Neoclassical Framework and the Nominal-Real Dichotomy

Absence of money illusion, the neutrality of money, as well as the so-called valid nominal-real dichotomy (see below), all stem from the basic homogeneity postulate: excess-demand functions in each and every market are homogeneous of degree zero in all nominal variables—that is, they are functions only of real (or *relative*-price) variables. General equilibrium will, in general, determine a unique solution for the real variables (and, with some Samuelsonian assumptions, also their stability). The price level, however, remains indeterminate unless one other nominal variable is fixed. This could be the money stock or the nominal wage or, in an open economy, the nominal exchange rate. This choice lies at the heart of the concept of a "nominal anchor."

In this context, one may invoke Patinkin's (1965) important distinction between the "invalid" and "valid" classical dichotomies: "It is fatal to succumb to the temptation to say that relative prices are determined in the commodity markets and absolute prices in the money market. This does not mean that value theory cannot be distinguished from monetary theory. Obviously, there is a distinction; but it is based on a dichotomization of *effects*, not on a dichotomization of *markets*" (Patinkin, 1965, p. 181). It is the latter, valid nominal-real dichotomy that is relevant for our present context.

Consider, first, a simplified closed-economy model that could conveniently be summarized in two excess-demand schedules for the labor and commodity markets respectively:

$$L(\underline{W/P}; A_\ell) = 0 \tag{1}$$

$$Y(\underset{+}{W/P}, \underset{+}{M/P}; A_y) = 0. \tag{2}$$

W, M, P are the nominal wage, aggregate money stock, and price level, respectively. A_ℓ and A_y are exogenous shift factors for the labor- and commodity-market excess-demand schedules (e.g., the capital stock and productivity; A_y also includes demand-shift factors like fiscal policy). The absence of the interest rate as a separate variable could be justified in terms of Patinkin's model (1965, chap. 9) through the substitution in the commodity market for the interest rate from the market equilibrium

9

condition for either money or bonds.[3] Equations (1) and (2) determine unique equilibria for the real wage (W/P) and real balances (M/P). Stability of the equilibrium depends, of course, on the conventional adjustment rules for W and P under excess demands L and Y.

Now, consider the simplest exercise in monetary expansion (we assume a static economy with no growth). An increase in money supply (M) causes an excess supply for money (not shown here) and an excess demand for goods (i.e., in equation 2, $Y > 0$). The inflationary gap brings about a dynamic adjustment in the price level (P moves up), which, in turn, reduces the real wage (at a given nominal wage W) and causes an excess demand for labor (in equation 1, $L > 0$). The latter, in turn, brings about a dynamic upward adjustment in W. Equilibrium will finally be reestablished only after P and W have increased at the same rate as the initial increase in M. As long as all markets (commodities as well as labor) are fully flexible, W and P levels will move toward a new unique equilibrium whenever M changes (whether upward or downward). These nominal magnitudes are bound to stay stable, however, if M is kept stable (as long, of course, as there is no change in the exogenous shift parameters A). It is in this sense that money is the nominal anchor of the system.

We might equally envisage an economy in which the nominal wage is the anchor. Suppose we are in a strongly unionized economy in which fear of Keynesian unemployment dictates an accommodating monetary policy. In that case, M/P will stay pegged and W will become the nominal anchor of the system. In the absence of price controls, a rise in W will eventually be followed by an equivalent increase in the price level (and the quantity of money), leaving relative prices (W/P and M/P) the same. Incomes policy (affecting W) will determine the relative stability of the system.

For the sake of completeness, we might ask if P itself can ever be directly controlled as the nominal anchor. The answer is a qualified

---

[3] In the original Patinkin model, M/P in the excess demand for goods comes from the real-balance effect. In this case, the interest rate appears as a separate variable, which could be suppressed by substitution from the equilibrium condition in the bond market. Thus, an alternative approach, based on an ISLM model tradition and leading to a similar formal result, would be the substitution for the interest rate in aggregate commodity demand Y from, for example, a money-equilibrium condition $H(M/P, i) = 0$ (in equilibrium, by Walras' Law, bonds will also be in equilibrium). Because investment (and consumption) demand depends on the *real* interest rate, one should in any case also include a price-expectations variable under the shift variable A_y. I am indebted to Carl Christ for pointing out an ambiguity in my previous version of this argument.

yes, provided we consider a command economy in which the prices of all components of the commodity basket (composing the aggregate index P) are fully controlled, as was the case in communist regimes of the old, and perhaps soon extinct, style. In such regimes, which presumably also dictate W across the economy, inflation, even if it potentially exists, will not come into the open. This may explain why, during periods of substantial open inflation in the Western industrial world, the Eastern Bloc countries have exhibited prolonged price stability.

An increase in M may cause excess demand for goods (in equation 2), and the inflationary gap will be bridged, not by price increases, but by shortages, rationing, queuing, and so forth. This is, in other words, a case of *repressed* inflation. In present-day Soviet Russia, the problem of the so-called "monetary overhang" is precisely that. Any price-liberalization process is bound to lead to open inflation. The price index, P, is thus a nominal anchor only in a very formal sense. The cost of recourse to such "anchoring" is a distortion of the real economy. Similarly, fixing W at a level that does not clear the labor market, if such a market exists at all, will force the system to disguise the level of unemployment.

Although an extreme form of sustained and widespread price and wage regulation may not seem a realistic possibility in a market economy, it should be pointed out that partial price and wage controls (e.g., controlled prices of key commodities and wage controls in the public sector) are rather widespread. The exercise of such controls in the process of stabilizing an economy, and even temporary imposition of full controls, could serve an important role in signaling expectations, provided, of course, that the real disequilibria are removed and fundamentals are first set in place. We shall come back to that question and the issue of "multiple" anchoring in Section 4.

Leaving aside the case of direct price or wage fixing, and as long as we are discussing a closed economy, we should agree that it is the quantity of money (or some other widely used nominal asset) that is the sole, and informationally the most efficient, nominal anchor of the system. Keynes, Patinkin, and most of the classical writers developed their macroeconomic frameworks for discussing monetary theory in the context of a closed economy. Neutrality of money and issues of price inflation were thus naturally centered on the control or loss of control over the money supply. Most economies of the world are open in one way or another, however, and the price system of one country can be tied to that of the rest of the world through the choice of the exchange rate. The exchange rate is, in theory at least, a perfectly valid contender to M as the centerpiece of the monetary game in any individual economy

11

(though not, of course, in the global economy, at least as long as there is no active trade with outer space).

The above macroeconomic framework is most easily and realistically extended into an open economy by allowing the aggregate good to be imperfectly tradeable on the export market (with exports positively dependent on exogenous world demand and relative world-to-domestic prices) while imports consist of a competing input into the aggregate production function. Equations (1) and (2) must now be rewritten with an additional relative price, the real exchange rate (E/P, in which E is the nominal exchange rate) appearing inside the respective excess-demand functions for labor and goods:[4]

$$L(W/P, E/P; A_\ell) = 0 \qquad (1')$$

$$Y(\underset{+}{W/P}, \underset{+}{M/P}, \underset{+}{E/P}; A_y). \qquad (2')$$

We now add a third market for foreign exchange with a suitable excess-demand function (the current account):

$$F(\underset{-}{E/P}, \underset{+}{W/P}; Y_f) = 0 \qquad (3)$$

The set of three equilibrium conditions (1'), (2'), and (3) will fix a unique solution for the three relative magnitudes M/P, W/P, and E/P, and fixing any one of the four nominal variables will fix the equilibrium level of the remaining three. The nominal exchange rate, E, is now a legitimate alternative nominal anchor. An exercise similar to the previous one can show how a change in E will feed into suitable changes in excess demands of other markets, and an adjustment in all other nominal variables will take place. The endogeneity of M in this simplified pegged exchange-rate system will come from a specie flow mechanism that feeds from changes in exchange reserves (when $F >$ or < 0) into the domestic money supply. The dynamic analysis must be suitably

---

[4] Because imports are an input into the production function, labor demand now depends also on the relative price, EP_n°/P, of the import good (P_n° is the world price of the import good that will appear as one of the components of the shift factor A_ℓ). A similar modification follows for the commodity market from both the supply and the demand side. Excess demand can be written as the difference between aggregate demand, $Y^d(\underset{+}{M/P}, \underset{-}{EP^\circ/P}; A_d)$, and aggregate supply, $Y^s(\underset{-}{M/P}, \underset{-}{EP_n^\circ/P}; A_s)$, in which P° is the world price of exports, and the shift factors are suitably extended to include the respective world parameters. The signs of response on E/P assume labor and imports to be gross substitutes in production.

12

modified if foreign-exchange borrowing is allowed and foreign and domestic assets are not perfect substitutes, but the long-run equilibrium solution is the same.

Price inflation has been represented so far as an adjustment to an excess demand in the commodity market, with parallel excess supply in the money (or foreign-exchange) market. A persistent inflationary process such as high inflation may very well continue even while the commodity market is in continuous balance. It will simplify matters if we make this assumption for the following discussion. Also, because we want to talk about high-inflation processes and comparative dynamics thereof, we can translate an equilibrium equation such as (2') into an equation in terms of rates of change of the nominal variables. We leave it to Section 3 to discuss the rationale for having the system sustain a steady rate of inflation at all.

Log-linearizing (1') and considering changes over time, we get

$$\pi = a_1\omega + a_2\varepsilon + a_3\mu + v, \tag{4}$$

in which $\pi = \dot{P}/P$ – rate of inflation, and a dot represents a discrete (P_t – P_{t-1}) or instantaneous (dP/dt) time change; $\omega = \dot{W}/W$ – wage inflation; $\varepsilon = \dot{E}/E$ – rate of devaluation; $\mu = \dot{M}/M$ – rate of monetary expansion; v – supply and demand shocks; $a_1 + a_2 + a_3 = 1$ by homogeneity of (1').

Equation (4) may be rewritten in the form of an *inflation-acceleration equation*:

$$\pi - \pi_{-1} = a_1(\omega - \pi_{-1}) + a_2(\varepsilon - \pi_{-1}) + a_3(\mu - \pi_{-1}) + v, \tag{5}$$

in which π_{-1} is the one-period lagged inflation rate $[(P_{t-1} - P_{t-2})/P_{t-1}]$.

Start from a steady state in which all nominal variables rise at the same rate μ_0. Suppose now that a real shock to the current account (e.g., A_f in equation 3 increases following a permanent fall in world demand) requires a step adjustment in the exchange rate that causes a one-time increase in E/P, that is, a one-time blip in $\varepsilon - \pi_{-1}$, after which, again, $\varepsilon = \pi$. In the absence of a negative real shift in the commodity market, such as a fiscal cut, this requires a one-time drop in M/P or in both M and P (simultaneous labor-market equilibrium would require both). If M and W have hitherto grown at the rate μ_0 and cannot be made to grow at a lower rate, only a one-time additional increase in the price level, causing a temporary blip to the inflation rate, will bring about the required one-time drop in M/P and W/P, after which all nominal magnitudes will resume their steady-state rate.

Suppose, however, money is always accommodating and wages are formally indexed to past inflation. In that case, $\omega = \mu = \pi_{-1}$ always. The

13

money stock, M, and nominal wage, W, will now grow at a rate higher than μ_0, after the devaluation. The one-time blip in $\varepsilon - \pi_{-1}$ in equation (5) (after which we must preserve $\varepsilon = \pi$) must cause a permanent increase in the inflation rate, and all nominal variables will rise at a new steady rate that is higher than μ_0. This, of course, is a well-known property of formally indexed systems that exhibit considerable inertia. Under full indexation, a one-time change in a relative price (real devaluation, real-wage and/or monetary cut) can only be achieved by a jump in the inflation rate itself.

An interesting property of such systems relates to workers' demand to raise the degree of indexation as the inflation rate increases but, at the same time, to reduce the length of lag in the formal part of indexation. Suppose wage adjustment takes the form $w = \delta\pi_{-1} + (1 - \delta)\pi^e$, in which π^e are the expectations of inflation as reflected in the wage contract, which also incorporates a partial cost of living adjustment (COLA). Accelerating inflation will tend to motivate an increase in δ that will enhance the inertia of the inflationary process. A shortening of the lag, however (embodied in the length of time between which π_{-1} and π are measured), actually reduces inertia. Monthly, weekly, and, in the limit, perhaps daily indexation will reduce inertia. It will also destroy the quasi stability of the process and enhance the shift from stage III (high inflation) to stage IV (hyperinflation). At the same time, reduced inertia will also facilitate the reduction of inflation, once the will is present, with relatively less real disruption.

3 Seigniorage and the Optimal Inflation Rate

We have avoided the question so far of a rationale for having any positive inflation rate. For that, we have to look at the rules governing the supply of and demand for the depreciable asset money. A natural beneficiary of inflation is the government, which reaps an inflation tax to the extent that the public is willing (or forced by law) to hold its depreciable monetary issue. Suppose we denote the part of the deficit financed by seigniorage by d, the nominal money base by H, and the real base (H/P) by h. In steady state, we have $\dot{H}/H = \pi$, the inflation rate, and therefore[5]

$$d = h\pi. \tag{6}$$

---

[5] Out of a steady state, we can write (for a discrete time model)
$d_t = (H_t - H_{t-1})/P_t = h_t - h_{t-1}(1 - \pi_t)$, in which $h_t = H_t/P_t$ and $\pi_t = (P_t - P_{t-1})/P_t$.

As is common in the literature and also confirmed by empirical work, assume a semi-log (Cagan, 1956) demand function for money, in which π^e denotes expected inflation (the real interest rate is assumed to be exogenous and is suppressed here).

$$h = \exp(-\alpha\pi^e). \tag{7}$$

Figure 3 draws equation (6) for a given d as a rectangular hyperbola and the money demand schedule h (equation 7) as cutting it, at most, at two points A and B, both of which represent steady-state inflationary equilibria ($\pi = \pi^e$). As is well known, there is one value of d at which there is a (single) tangent point between the two curves. This is Friedman's (1971) maximum seigniorage (d^0):

$$d^0 = \text{Max}[\pi \exp(-\alpha\pi)] = 1/\alpha e,$$

in which the maximizing inflation rate is $\pi^0 = 1/\alpha$.

The elasticity of demand for money ($\alpha\pi$) at that point is unity. If $d > d^0$, there is no steady-state equilibrium (this may correspond to the case of explosive hyperinflation), whereas, for $d < d^0$, there will be two

FIGURE 3

GOVERNMENT FINANCE, MONETARY BASE, AND EQUILIBRIUM INFLATION

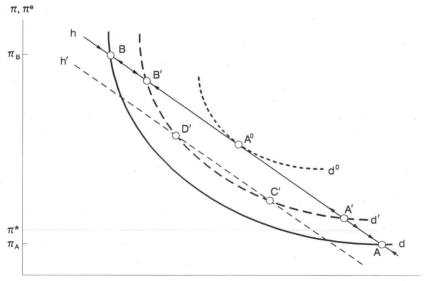

intersections, A and B, as shown in Figure 3.

Rightward shifts of the d curve (an increase in the seigniorage finance deficit) or leftward shifts of the money-demand function (a fall in money demand or a rise in an exogenously given reserve ratio) will cause an upward shift of the lower equilibrium point A, that is, an increase in steady-state inflation. In a growth context (with rate of growth n), d should be taken as the share in GNP, and, in that case, equation (6) becomes $d = (\pi + n)h$; the curve could also shift to the right by an exogenous drop in the rate of growth.

The above framework has been used to rationalize the upward jumps in Israel's inflation profile in the 1970-85 period (see Bruno and Fischer, 1986). Empirical evidence for Israel in the period (Melnick and Sokoler, 1984) also suggests that the revenue-maximizing rate was 6.5 percent a month (115-percent annual inflation) and that, starting somewhere around the early 1980s, the elasticity of demand for money exceeded unity and inflation may have moved toward an upper (B) equilibrium. Note that, at B, an increase in the deficit actually *reduces* the inflation rate—a perverse result that will be discussed below.

Is there a sense in which an upper, high-inflation equilibrium could be rationalized as the outcome of optimal choice? An argument based on Barro (1983)[6] clearly suggests there is, provided we assume discretionary behavior. Suppose we assume that the government benefits from seigniorage but trades off that benefit against the social costs of both actual (π) and anticipated (π^e) inflation. Assume that the objective function takes the general form

$$V = \sigma d - f(\pi) - g(\pi^e),\tag{8}$$

in which σ (the marginal benefit from seigniorage) is exogenous but may vary over time, and f', $g' > 0$.

Substituting from equations (6) and (7) into (8) and maximizing V with respect to π (choosing actual money growth for given π^e), we find

$$V'_\pi \big|_{\pi^e} = \sigma \exp(-\alpha\pi^e) - f'(\pi) = 0.\tag{9}$$

Under rational expectations on the part of the private sector, we have $\pi = \pi^e$. This gives an equilibrium inflation rate that may very well be at a point like B.

From equation (9), we have in discretionary equilibrium π_d:

---

[6] I am indebted to Nissan Liviatan for this reference. See also Kiguel and Liviatan (1990).

16

$$\alpha\pi_d = \ell n\sigma - \ell nf'(\pi_d). \tag{10}$$

For sufficiently large σ, $\alpha\pi_d$ will be > 1.[7]

In theory, at least, this presents an interesting paradox. With an economy at a stable high-inflation equilibrium (B in Figure 3), a mere budget cut (leftward shift of the d curve) will shift the new B equilibrium up—that is, in the absence of a change in the dynamic-adjustment rules, the new upper-equilibrium inflation rate is even higher. This seeming paradox can be given economic content (see Bruno, 1989): the fiscal cut involves an instantaneous monetary squeeze and a step increase in the nominal interest rate, with asset markets adjusting instantaneously and the commodity market more slowly. An upward shift in the interest rate signals an equal shift in $\varepsilon_t - \varepsilon_{t-1}$ and in inflationary expectations.

The vagaries of discretion stand out even more when we contrast its use with the alternative case of a government that can precommit itself and thus control inflationary expectations in a nondiscretionary ("rule-determined") way. If one maximizes V under precommitment ($\pi = \pi^e$), we get

$$V'\big|_{\pi=\pi^e} = (1 - \alpha\pi)\sigma \exp(-\alpha\pi) - f'(\pi) - g'(\pi) = 0. \tag{11}$$

For this equilibrium rate (denoted by π_R), we have

$$1 - \alpha\pi_R = \frac{\exp(\alpha\pi_R)}{\sigma(f' + g')} > 0.$$

Thus, *the optimal precommitted rate of inflation will always be less than the revenue-maximizing rate*, that is, the economy will, under precommitment, always be at a low equilibrium point like A.[8]

One weakness of the preceding analysis is the assumption that d itself is chosen in some optimal way. Another is related to the stability of the equilibrium inflation rate. In practice, governments often find themselves in deficits or in inflationary situations as a result of past mistakes, and they stay there because they are unable to muster the strength or the social consensus needed for a major reform. Suppose,

---

[7] For example, using an exponential form for f (as in Barro, 1983), we get an explicit analytical solution. Assuming $f(\pi) = k/b \exp(b\pi)$, we get $\pi_d = \ell n(\sigma/k)/(b + \alpha)$. Thus $\alpha\pi_d > 1$ provided $\sigma > k \exp(1 + b/\alpha)$.

[8] Note that we get zero inflation, ($\pi_R = 0$), when $f'(\pi_R) + g'(\pi_R) = 1/\sigma$. Also note that this result does not depend on the inclusion of $g(\pi^e)$ in the objective function V, that is, one may put $g' \equiv 0$ in equation (11).

now, that d is exogenously determined and that we ask what determines the stability of an equilibrium point A or B. For that, we have to say something about expectation formation or dynamic behavior of the nominal variables out of steady-state equilibrium. The avenues that have been studied all have some friction in the inflationary process, whether in adjustment of price expectations, money, wages, or exchange rates. The speed of adjustment determines the stability or instability of equilibrium at A or B.

The simplest example, for a closed economy, is that of adaptive expectations (see Bruno and Fischer, 1990):

$$\dot{\pi}^e = \beta(\pi - \pi^e). \tag{12}$$

Log time-differentiation of equation (7) and substitution in (12) gives the equation of motion of π^e out of equilibrium:

$$\dot{\pi}^e = (1 - \alpha\beta)^{-1}\beta[d \exp(\alpha\pi^e) - \pi^e]. \tag{13}$$

The familiar Cagan Condition (1956) $\alpha\beta < 1$ or > 1 determines whether A, B are stable or unstable equilibria, respectively. It is important to point out that adaptive adjustment of expectations is only one option by which this result is obtained. Slow adjustment of one of the other nominal magnitudes under rational expectations will give similar results. In another paper (Bruno, 1989), I have applied the same idea to the exchange rate, substituting ε (the rate of devaluation) for π^e in equations (7) and (12). Another modification makes the adjustment coefficient (β) increase with the rate of inflation. This is a rule for a crawling peg that has also been estimated empirically:

$$\dot{\varepsilon} = \beta(\pi)(\pi - \varepsilon). \tag{14}$$

The variability of β raises the interesting possibility that both A and B may be stable equilibria. Assume $\beta'(\pi) > 0$, and let $\pi*$ be the threshold inflation rate at which $\alpha\beta(\pi*) = 1$. If $\pi_A < \pi* < \pi_B$, both equilibria are, in fact, stable.

A discrete time version (nonlinear difference equation) was run over 123 monthly observations for the crawling-peg period in Israel from 1975 to 1985 in the form

$$\varepsilon_t - \varepsilon_{t-1} = \beta_0 - (\beta_1 + \beta_2\pi_{t-1})(\pi_{t-1} - \pi_{t-1}^{US} - \varepsilon_{t-1}) + J_t,$$

in which π^{US} is the U.S. inflation rate and J_t are dummy (jump) variables for periods of discrete-level devaluations that took place in 1975, 1977, and 1983. The threshold inflation rate ($\pi*$) was estimated to be a monthly rate of 4.8 percent for wholesale prices or 5.8 percent for

18

consumer prices, 76 and 97 percent, respectively, in annual terms (Bruno, 1989). This is the rate that roughly distinguishes between two-digit (stage II) and three-digit (stage III) high inflations.

Can an adjustment rule like equation (14) be motivated through an underlying optimization? It can, if one takes the existence of inflation as a norm.[9] Because a steady process of inflation has already been taking place, there are costs of marginally deviating from it. Some local suboptimization may therefore still be relevant. Assume the government minimizes a quadratic loss function of the form

$$L_t = \alpha_1(\varepsilon_t - \varepsilon_{t-1})^2 + \alpha_2(\omega_t - \varepsilon_t - \alpha_0)^2. \qquad (15)$$

The first term represents the cost, not of inflation per se, but of changes thereof, while the second represents the cost of deviations from current-account balance (depending on the relative exchange rate). It does not matter whether we replace ω_t by π_{t-1} or by π_t^e, as long as it is exogenous to the choice of ε_t.

Maximizing L_t with respect to ε_t, we get

$$\varepsilon_t - \varepsilon_{t-1} = \beta(\omega_t - \varepsilon_t - \alpha_0), \qquad (16)$$

in which $\beta = \alpha_2/\alpha_1$. This is precisely the discretionary adjustment rule that was introduced above and observed in the empirical data, except that we have now provided a rationale for it. It also makes sense to assume that the higher the rate of inflation, the smaller will be the marginal cost of absolute deviations from it relative to those of current-account imbalance. Thus, β may be assumed to rise with the rate of inflation.[10] A weakness of the quadratic loss function (equation 15) is its symmetry with respect to upward and downward deviations.

It is interesting to note that such suboptimization may anchor the rate of inflation at either a higher or lower inflation rate depending on initial conditions and external inflationary shocks to the system. The two alternative equilibria themselves, however, depend on real fundamentals.

The sharp rise in Israel's inflation rate between 1975 and 1980 can be attributed by this theory to two major monetary decisions. The one on which many observers agree is the introduction of foreign-exchange-

---

[9] I am indebted to Nissan Liviatan for this important insight.
[10] The rate of change of W/E is $\omega - \varepsilon$, that is, the rate of real appreciation, which leads to a change in foreign-exchange reserves. The absolute change in the rate of devaluation (inflation) is $\varepsilon_t - \varepsilon_{t-1}$. At a steady rate of inflation of 100 percent per annum, a 5-percent deviation is relatively less costly than the same absolute deviation at a 10-percent steady rate.

19

linked bank accounts in 1977-78. This has shifted the demand for M_1 (an inward shift in the h schedule in Figure 3) and introduced indexation into a broader measure of money M_3. The other, much less stressed decision is that taken in 1975 to give up the pegged foreign-exchange-rate anchor and move to a flexible crawling peg. Gottlieb and Piterman (1985) identified 1975 as a crucial turning point in the expectation-formation mechanism. This amounts to a change from $\beta = 0$ in equation (14) to $\beta > 0$ and gradually rising.

A discrete devaluation in 1977, and again in 1983, caused not only a jump in the price level, but, with almost complete indexation of the nominal system, a series of upward jumps in the rate of inflation ("flats" in terms of Figure 2), making the system tend to move toward higher inflation equilibria. A new equilibrium was probably never reached after the 1983 shock, because the 1985 stabilization interrupted the process.

4 Choice of Anchors during Disinflation

Consider a country that has been running a high inflation and that wishes to stabilize while minimizing the initial cost of adjustment. First and foremost, the real source of fundamental disequilibrium has to be removed. The existence or absence of that necessary "orthodox" ingredient was the major distinction between success and failure in recent stabilization episodes of the 1980s. We therefore assume that the policy package includes a set of measures that corrects the fundamental sources of imbalance in the government budget or the balance of payments or, usually, in both. This would generally involve a substantial fiscal cut with or without an initial step adjustment in the exchange rate. Our discussion here, however, takes off from the point that the correction of fundamentals will usually not suffice to eliminate high inflation. Our earlier analysis tells us that the corrected real system could still be consistent with more than one inflation rate, and the self-perpetuating nominal mechanism must for that reason be made to switch at once to a stable low- (or zero-) inflation target. Minimizing the social cost of adjustment (or even enabling its political feasibility), moreover, dictates minimal superfluous changes in *relative* prices during the transition.

There are at least two separate issues here. One is the problem created by formal institutional arrangements such as backward indexation, particularly of wages. Even if inflation starts to drop, lagged indexation may cause a very large initial increase in the real wage and

20

thus exacerbate unemployment. The nominal system must be made to forget its memory of the past. But a mere formal de-indexation will in general not suffice either, for sluggish change in government credibility (or lack of price coordination) may cause forward nominal stickiness (in ω and π). A clear signal of a sharp shift in policy is required, by targeting at least one nominal anchor (the possible need for more than one anchor will be taken up below). Suppose one central anchor has to be pegged during the transition to low inflation. Is it the exchange rate or the quantity of money?

The Argument in Favor of the Exchange Rate

The cumulative history of sharp disinflations in open economies points to a dominant use of the exchange rate as a key nominal anchor. Dornbusch (1986) gave a general discussion of its role in stabilization in an earlier Graham Lecture. In a survey of past substantial inflations (Yeager, 1981), only the Italian disinflation of 1945 seems to have involved extensive use of a monetary target rather than the exchange rate. In almost all historical hyperinflations as well as in recent attempts at stabilization from high inflation, fixing the exchange was a key element of rapid stabilization (see Dornbusch and Fischer, 1986; Bruno et al., 1988, 1991). In the case of more moderate inflations, the experience is more mixed (see Kiguel and Liviatan, 1989).

There are several practical reasons for choosing the exchange rate, quite apart from the intuitive reasoning that, if the exchange rate had been a key manifestation of the loss of the nominal anchor, it would only make sense that disinflation would require its reestablishment. But is there a more systematic theoretical argument for the choice?

Fischer (1986) has investigated the question in the context of a small open economy (of the kind mentioned in Section 2) with perfect capital mobility and wage contracts set for either one or two periods, thus explicitly bringing in some nominal stickiness but no backward indexation. His model assumes rational expectations and instantaneous credibility once a policy change takes place (a highly questionable assumption in practice that will be discussed again below). Exchange-rate-led stabilization is compared with that led by a money-growth target in terms of the resulting sacrifice ratio, the ratio of total loss of output to the fall in the inflation rate, calculated over two periods.

The analysis shows that, although examples of exceptions can be produced, the case of exchange-rate stabilization is in general less costly. For the same drop in the inflation rate, the fall in the quantity of money is smaller under reduced exchange-rate adjustment (because

21

endogenous money demand rises as a result of the drop in ε, here the interest rate). The required equivalent reduction in the money-growth rate under the monetary option (with a flexible exchange rate) is thus larger. With a smaller reduction in the quantity of money, given wage stickiness, the output loss is smaller. The extent of the recession depends on wage stickiness and sensitivity of aggregate demand to the real exchange rate (which appreciates) and the real interest rate (which rises), and, for this reason, the result is not unambiguous. Fischer shows one extreme example in which exchange-rate stabilization produces a higher sacrifice ratio than money-growth stabilization—when interest elasticity of money demand is zero (i.e., extremely low), and the direct elasticity of the price level to exchange-rate changes in the cost function is very high (0.8 is assumed), both of which are empirically unlikely.

A larger recession with monetary stabilization could, in principle, be avoided if the reduction in the *rate of growth* of money is coupled with a one-time initial upward adjustment in the *level* of the money stock. Such up-front monetary expansion would create a well-known credibility problem, however, and is therefore inadvisable.

Once uncertainty is introduced into the analysis, the specific market location of disturbances affects the result. If disturbances arise in the goods market, output tends to be less stable under a fixed exchange rate than under fixed money, whereas prices tend to be less stable under a fixed money rule. What is probably more relevant in practice is the finding that the fixed-exchange-rate regime is preferable when disturbances are primarily in the demand for money, a fact well born out in the practice of stabilization. Wage disturbances are a problem under either procedure and provide the rationale for making wages consistent with the new inflation target through an incomes policy or a "package deal," a subject to which we shall return below.

Howitt (1987) has analyzed a model similar to Fischer's (1986) in which he discusses the optimal disinflation policies of a central bank under two types of wage-stickiness assumptions, backward-looking stickiness under a dynamic Phillips curve and forward-looking stickiness arising from lack of credibility. A history of positive inflation is assumed and a disinflation program is instituted. The central bank is presumed to maximize an infinite sum of squared output and inflation terms. Under backward stickiness, the optimal speed of disinflation becomes an increasing function of the weight attached to inflation in the objective function and of the slope of the Phillips curve. Monotonic reduction of monetary expansion is found to be not generally optimal. Rather E/P should be reduced immediately and then allowed to rise monotonically back to its initial value. A similar general result is obtained under forward stickiness coming from lack of credibility—the government has no tolerance of inflation but private agents do not know this. The speed of disinflation depends on a variance ratio that measures the severity of the central bank's credibility problem.

In practice, the problem of credibility encourages relatively "soft" governments to attach themselves to the reputation of a "stronger" government's conservative central bank through a fixed exchange rate. Historically inflation-prone countries, like Italy and France, adopted this strategy to join the EMS and tie themselves to a strong deutsche mark (see Giavazzi and Giovannini, 1989). The United Kingdom, by contrast, delayed its decision to enter the EMS and suffered from a considerably higher inflation rate, though for nonfiscal reasons. It will be interesting to see how the United Kingdom's entry into the EMS in October 1990 will have affected its subsequent relative inflation performance.

In addition to the theoretical arguments discussed above, there are several quasi-practical advantages of choosing the exchange rate over the money supply in the process of disinflation. In an open economy, tradeable goods form a substantial part of the goods basket and thus of the components of the price level. Stabilizing a key price in the economy, which is observable on a daily basis (unlike the price index, usually published once a month and with some delay), thus provides a more important and clearer signal to the rest of the system than the indirect signal embodied in the quantity of money. The exchange rate is also a clearer magnitude to set against the wage rate in the stabilization game played with the wage fixers, whether employers or unions, in a highly unionized economy (see following subsection). Finally, the instability of monetary targets, especially during disinflations, has already been mentioned. The demand for M_1, for one, tends to rise steeply in the early stages of a quick disinflation as expected inflation is adjusted downward.

We have not discussed here the basis for exchange-rate pegging during transition to lower inflation, but it may be of considerable practical importance. Pegging to a major currency substituting for domestic money in the asset market and thus serving as a unit of account in many transactions would be preferable from the point of view of establishing initial credibility (the dollar in the case of Israel and the deutsche mark in the recent stabilizations of Yugoslavia and Poland). Pegging to a trade-weighted basket of currencies would be preferable from the point of view of real trade flows, given the fluctuations of cross rates in world markets. Israel, in fact, moved to a basket approximately one year after its initial stabilization.

23

Multiple Nominal Anchors

If the exchange rate seems a more effective instrument than money supply, what are its defects? The key problem arises from forward wage and price stickiness resulting from the slow buildup in credibility. This stickiness invariably leads to real appreciation of the exchange rate and expectations of further adjustment of the exchange-rate peg, resulting in large cycles of speculative capital flows and substantial monetary and interest-rate fluctuations. To avoid regime collapse, larger exchange reserves must be held under this regime than under a flexible exchange rate, and there is also a tendency to maintain exchange controls that can be distortive or relatively ineffective.

These arguments suggest the wisdom of using the exchange rate as a key anchor in the early stages of sharp stabilization but of moving in the direction of a more flexible exchange rate once credibility has been developed. For example, the median exchange rate can be kept as a longer-run signal while greater short-run fluctuations within a fixed band are allowed. This would enable a moderation of capital movements and provide a more active role for monetary policy even under less restrictive foreign-exchange controls.

Does it pay to coordinate more than one anchor in the process of disinflation? To answer the question, one should distinguish between the two possible stages in the stabilization process: the initial step of a very sharp cut in inflation (from three-digit inflation to 20 percent per annum, for example) and the subsequent, usually slower and more gradual, drop to the lowest (zero?) inflation target.

Assume as before that the required fiscal and exchange-rate adjustments have been made and that the exchange rate is now pegged. Even the smallest backward or forward stickiness in any of the other nominal aggregates in a disinflating system with confusing signals may cause very sharp shifts in *relative* prices, which may in turn upset the planned equilibrium of the real system. Wage indexation has to be suspended, at least temporarily, and monetary aggregates had better be set to be consistent with the wage and exchange-rate freeze. Are temporary price controls—the fourth anchor—also required? Given the uncertainty of signals, especially for nontradeable goods and services (wages in the government service sector, for example), price controls can help in signaling the sudden shift and absolute commitment of the new policy. An across-the-board freeze of prices may be required as part of the bargain anyway in making a deal with the trade unions on a wage freeze (this was the experience in the Israeli stabilization of

1985). Price controls, if they are to be monitored by the public, can only apply to an absolute-level freeze, and not to any positive rate of inflation, which cannot be easily monitored.

We know that controls can be very distortionary, but a sharp disinflation, if it persists, may outweigh the temporary distortive effects of price controls in terms of the distortions eliminated. This argument suggests, however, that price controls may not pay for small disinflations, and they had better be short-lived and eliminated rather quickly even under large disinflations, as soon as the credibility and signaling objective has been achieved.

Given the underlying macroeconomic framework of Section 2, an argument that calls for the fixing of more than one nominal variable at a time is *prima facie* contradictory. The system must be overdetermined or, alternatively, fall into a disequilibrium unless the coordinated choice of nominal targets is exactly right. This conclusion, however, rests on an assumption of full certainty. Here, we are considering an optimal policy choice under uncertainty, in which market equilibrium or disequilibrium must be redefined in an expectational sense. Given the potential benefits of success and the high risks of failure of a sharp disinflation, tying one's boat to several anchors would seem to be a prudent policy, as would be portfolio diversification of risk in the optimal menu of risky assets.

The analogue of multiple anchoring (in which only one of the ropes can be tight and may threaten to break at any time) was the rationale behind the simultaneous intervention in all other nominal variables during the Israeli stabilization of 1985. In addition to a sharp fiscal contraction (including a cut in subsidies) and an up-front devaluation, the government announced a credit freeze as well as its intention to keep the exchange rate pegged—if the unions would temporarily suspend the COLA and freeze wages for a few months. Agreement on the latter was, in turn, made conditional on the introduction of price controls. The resulting tripartite agreement between employers, trade unions, and government provided the supportive means by which the nominal system was at once shifted from a 500-percent inflation to 25 percent (and, subsequently, 15 to 20 percent) per annum.

It is important to point out that the *ex ante* freeze of all nominal variables other than the exchange rate was rather short-lived *ex post*, and significant changes took place in *relative* prices only a few months after the initial shock, primarily in a real-wage increase and a real appreciation. Yet, the lower inflation rate was successfully maintained. This success may show that the signaling of serious intentions and

25

precommitment on the part of the government constituted the most important role of the synchronized freeze in the early stage of stabilization. A real appreciation (though not a real-wage increase) has also accompanied the successful stabilization in Bolivia and Mexico.

Consider now the second stage. Once price controls are lifted and the exchange rate is maintained as the key nominal anchor, monetary policy will be geared to protect the exchange rate. The inflation that remains can best be described as the outcome of a repeated game between the government (setting the exchange rate) and the private sector (setting the nominal wage), in which the government attempts to establish its reputation, and credibility is gradually developed. In practice, the game may be much more complicated, with each sector also playing an internal game: the central bank versus the ministry of finance over the commitment to a pegged exchange rate; the unions versus the employers over the wage rate. Even the case of the bilateral monopoly is not easy to model realistically, however, although a beginning has been made in a paper by Horn and Persson (1988).

In Israel, the exchange rate was adjusted five times during the five years following the July 1985 stabilization (January 1987, December 1988, January 1989, June 1989, and March 1990), changes almost always coupled with an agreed-upon suspension of the COLA. Since March 1990, Israel has moved to a more flexible regime in which fluctuations within a 5-percent band above and below the mid-rate are allowed and a greater role in the determination of the exchange rate is given to the foreign-exchange market and to monetary policy. An alignment of the mid-rate was made in September 1990 and in March 1991.

Table 3 shows the annual rates of change of the nominal exchange rate (trade-weighted basket of currencies), the nominal wage, and the per unit real-wage costs in the business sector. The figures suggest a gradual learning process in nominal wage behavior over the period from 1985 to 1990, with an eventual turnaround in unit real-wage costs in 1988 and a possible further drop in inflation by the end of the period. This result, however, was bought at the cost of rising unemployment and considerable initial real appreciation. A more flexible foreign-exchange market and the slack in the labor market now allow a gradual easing away from the exchange rate as a single nominal anchor. A sequence of exchange-rate realignments, with real appreciations as well as painful adjustments of management and labor, have also characterized the gradual and very slow disinflations of EMS-linked countries like Italy and France over the 1980s. Because of its much more flexible labor market, Mexico could shift from a fixed peg to a crawling devalu-

ation at an earlier stage in its stabilization program, albeit at a rate that
has kept real appreciation going.

TABLE 3

THE EXCHANGE RATE, NOMINAL WAGE, AND PER UNIT REAL-WAGE
COSTS IN THE BUSINESS SECTOR IN ISRAEL, 1986-1990
(annual rate of change)

	1986	1987	1988	1989	1990
Exchange rate [a]	45	13	2	16	11
Nominal wage	65	33	22	18	15
Unit real-wage costs	6	4	-2	-1	0
Rate of unemployment	7%	6%	6%	9%	10%
Product prices [b]	51	19	18	19	12
Consumer prices [c]	53	20	16	18	13

SOURCE: Bank of Israel, 1991.
[a] Based on a trade-weighted basket of currencies.
[b] Implicit price index of GDP in the business sector.
[c] Cost of living index excluding housing prices.

The second phase of a disinflation process, the gradual reduction of
a 20- to 25-percent inflation rate, is the most difficult part of the
stabilization effort. In all recent successful stabilizations, in Israel,
Bolivia, Chile, and Mexico, the inflation rate has remained close to that
range. The stickiness of the rate in all of these cases has most probably
been related to a lack of credibility and the weakening of commitment
to the goal of stability once "the worst" was seemingly over. In Israel's
case, a variety of structural factors (slow removal of indexation, slow
dismantling of protective and monopolistic obstacles, minimum-real-
wage legislation, etc.) played an inhibiting role. Of the above four
countries, only Chile has managed in recent years to reverse the trend
in its real exchange rate.

In characterizing the end of the high-inflation process, we may also
return to the issue of the nominal-real dichotomy. The system undergoes
a fundamental change in this respect as inflation "lifts off" from a two-
digit range into a high-inflation dichotomous regime. Once sharp
disinflation has taken place, one may expect in the "re-entry" phase a
reversal of the dichotomy between the nominal and the real economy
and a closer resemblance to the ordinary garden-variety inflations. One
would thus expect to see much less nominal accommodation and an
enhanced importance of real versus nominal shocks. A related property
would be an increase in the tradeoff between inflation and unemploy-

27

ment, which virtually disappears under high inflation. A recent study by Leiderman and Liviatan (1989) confirms these findings for a comparison of the behavior of nominal and real variables in Israel before and after stabilization. The degree of nominal inertia has substantially fallen, whereas the variability of changes in real output, employment, and the trade deficit has not changed. The Phillips curve short-term tradeoff seems to have increased considerably. This is further evidence for a shift back from stage III (high chronic) inflation to a lower-stage inflation regime. It remains to be seen if and when the economy of Israel, and, similarly, the economies of Bolivia, Chile, and Mexico, will finally move to the lower rate of inflation that has characterized the industrial world in recent years.

References

Bank of Israel, *Annual Report 1990*, Jerusalem, May 1991.

Barro, Robert J., "Inflationary Finance Under Discretion and Rules," *Canadian Journal of Economics*, 16 (No. 1, February 1983), pp. 1-16.

Bruno, Michael, "Econometrics and the Design of Economic Reform," *Econometrica*, 57 (No. 2, March 1989), pp. 275-306.

Bruno, Michael, Guido Di Tella, Rudiger Dornbusch, and Stanley Fischer, eds., *Inflation Stabilization: The Experience of Israel, Argentina, Brazil, Bolivia, and Mexico*, Cambridge, Mass., MIT Press, 1988.

Bruno, Michael, and Stanley Fischer, "The Inflationary Process: Shocks and Accommodation," in Yoram Ben-Porath, ed., *The Israeli Economy: Maturing through Crises*, Cambridge, Mass., Harvard University Press, 1986, pp. 347-371.

———, "Seignorage, Operating Rules and the High Inflation Trap," *Quarterly Journal of Economics*, 105 (No. 421, May 1990), pp. 353-374.

Bruno, Michael, Stanley Fischer, Elhanan Helpman, and Nissan Liviatan, eds., *Lessons of Economic Stabilization and its Aftermath*, Cambridge, Mass., MIT Press, forthcoming, 1991.

Cagan, Phillip, "The Monetary Dynamics of Hyperinflation," in Milton Friedman, ed., *Studies in the Quantity Theory of Money*, Chicago, Chicago University Press, 1956, pp. 117-225.

Dornbusch, Rudiger, *Inflation, Exchange Rates, and Stabilization*, Essays in International Finance No. 165, Princeton, N.J., Princeton University, International Finance Section, October 1986.

Dornbusch, Rudiger, and Stanley Fischer, "Stopping Hyperinflation: Past and Present," *Weltwirtschaftliches Archiv*, 122 (1986), pp. 1-47.

Fischer, Stanley, "Exchange Rates versus Money Targets in Disinflation," in Stanley Fischer, ed., *Indexing, Inflation, and Economic Policy*, Cambridge, Mass., MIT Press, 1986, pp. 247-262.

Friedman, Milton, "Government Revenue from Inflation," *Journal of Political Economy*, 79 (1971), pp. 846-857.

Giavazzi, Francesco, and Alberto Giovannini, *Limiting Exchange Rate Flexibility: The European Monetary System*, Cambridge, Mass., MIT Press, 1989.

Gottlieb, Daniel, and Sylvia Piterman, "Inflationary Expectations in Israel," *Bank of Israel Economic Review*, 57 (May 1985), pp. 1-25.

Graham, Frank D., *Exchange, Prices, and Production in Hyper-Inflation: Germany, 1920-23*, Princeton, N.J., Princeton University Press, 1930.

Horn, Henrik, and Torsten Persson, "Exchange Rate Policy, Wage Formation and Credibility," *European Economic Review*, 32 (October 1988), pp. 1621-1636.

Howitt, Peter, "Optimal Disinflation in a Small Open Economy," University of Western Ontario, July 1987, processed.

Kiguel, Miguel, and Nissan Liviatan, "The Old and New in Heterodox Stabilization Programs: Lessons from the Sixties and the Eighties," *The World Bank Economic Review* (forthcoming 1991).

————, "Some Implications of Policy Games for High Inflation Economies," World Bank Working Paper No. 379, Washington, D.C., The World Bank, March 1990.

Leiderman, Leonardo, and Nissan Liviatan, "Macroeconomic Performance before and after Disinflation in Israel," World Bank Working Paper No. 311, Washington, D.C., The World Bank, August 1989.

Liviatan, Nissan, "Inflation and the Composition of Deficit Finance," in Francis G. Adams and Bert G. Hickman, eds., *Global Econometrics*, Cambridge, Mass., MIT Press, 1983.

Melnick, Raphael, and Meir Sokoler, "The Government's Revenue Creation and the Inflationary Effect of a Decline in the Rate of Growth of GNP," *Journal of Monetary Economics*, 13 (1984), pp. 225-236.

Patinkin, Don, *Money, Interest and Prices*, New York, Harper and Row, 1965.

Pazos, Felipe, *Chronic Inflation in Latin America*, New York, Praeger, 1972.

Sargent, Thomas J., "The Ends of Four Big Inflations," in Robert E. Hall, ed., *Inflation: Causes and Effects*, Chicago and London, University of Chicago Press, 1982, pp. 41-97.

Sargent, Thomas J., and Neil Wallace, "Inflation and the Government Budget Constraint," in Assaf Razin and Efraim Sadka, eds., *Economic Policy in Theory and Practice*, Basingstoke, Macmillan, 1987.

Willis, Henry P., and Benjamin H. Beckhart, eds., *Foreign Banking Systems*, New York, Henry Holt, 1929.

Yeager, Leland B., *Experiences with Stopping Inflation*, Washington, D.C., American Enterprise Institute for Public Policy Research, 1981.

29

FRANK D. GRAHAM MEMORIAL LECTURERS

1950–1951	Milton Friedman
1951–1952	James E. Meade
1952–1953	Sir Dennis Robertson
1953–1954	Paul A. Samuelson
1955–1956	Gottfried Haberler
1956–1957	Ragnar Nurkse
1957–1958	Albert O. Hirschman
1959–1960	Robert Triffin
1960–1961	Jacob Viner
1961–1962	Don Patinkin
1962–1963	Friedrich A. Lutz (Essay 41)
1963–1964	Tibor Scitovsky (Essay 49)
1964–1965	Sir John Hicks
1965–1966	Robert A. Mundell
1966–1967	Jagdish N. Bhagwati (Special Paper 8)
1967–1968	Arnold C. Harberger
1968–1969	Harry G. Johnson
1969–1970	Richard N. Cooper (Essay 86)
1970–1971	W. Max Corden (Essay 93)
1971–1972	Richard E. Caves (Special Paper 10)
1972–1973	Paul A. Volcker
1973–1974	J. Marcus Fleming (Essay 107)
1974–1975	Anne O. Krueger (Study 40)
1975–1976	Ronald W. Jones (Special Paper 12)
1976–1977	Ronald I. McKinnon (Essay 125)
1977–1978	Charles P. Kindleberger (Essay 129)
1978–1979	Bertil Ohlin (Essay 134)
1979–1980	Bela Balassa (Essay 141)
1980–1981	Marina von Neumann Whitman (Essay 143)
1981–1982	Robert E. Baldwin (Essay 150)
1983–1984	Stephen Marris (Essay 155)
1984–1985	Rudiger Dornbusch (Essay 165)
1986–1987	Jacob A. Frenkel (Study 63)
1987–1988	Ronald Findlay (Essay 177)
1988–1989	Michael Bruno (Essay 183)
1988–1989	Elhanan Helpman (Special Paper 16)
1989–1990	Michael L. Mussa (Essay 179)

PUBLICATIONS OF THE
INTERNATIONAL FINANCE SECTION

Notice to Contributors

The International Finance Section publishes papers in four series: ESSAYS IN INTER-NATIONAL FINANCE, PRINCETON STUDIES IN INTERNATIONAL FINANCE, SPECIAL PAPERS IN INTERNATIONAL ECONOMICS, AND REPRINTS IN INTERNATIONAL FINANCE. ESSAYS, STUDIES, AND SPECIAL PAPERS contain new work not published elsewhere. REPRINTS reproduce journal articles previously published by Princeton faculty members associated with the Section. The Section welcomes the submission of manuscripts for publication under the following guidelines:

ESSAYS are meant to disseminate new views about international financial matters and should be accessible to well-informed nonspecialists as well as to professional economists. Technical terms, tables, and charts should be used sparingly; mathematics should be avoided.

STUDIES are devoted to new research on international finance, with preference given to empirical work. They should be comparable in originality and technical proficiency to papers published in leading economic journals. They should be of medium length, longer than a journal article but shorter than a book.

SPECIAL PAPERS are surveys of research on particular topics and should be suitable for use in undergraduate courses. They may be concerned with international trade as well as international finance. They should also be of medium length.

Manuscripts should be submitted in triplicate, typed single sided and double spaced throughout on 8½ by 11 white bond paper. Publication can be expedited if manuscripts are computer keyboarded in WordPerfect 5.1 or a compatible program. Additional instructions and a style guide are available from the Section.

How to Obtain Publications

The Section's publications are distributed free of charge to college, university, and public libraries and to nongovernmental, nonprofit research institutions. Eligible institutions may ask to be placed on the Section's permanent mailing list.

Individuals and institutions not qualifying for free distribution may receive all publications for the calendar year for a subscription fee of $30.00. Late subscribers will receive all back issues for the year during which they subscribe. Subscribers should notify the Section promptly of any change in address, giving the old address as well as the new.

Publications may be ordered individually, with payment made in advance. ESSAYS and REPRINTS cost $6.50 each; STUDIES and SPECIAL PAPERS cost $9.00. An additional $1.25 should be sent for postage and handling within the United States, Canada, and Mexico; $1.50 should be added for surface delivery outside the region.

All payments must be made in U.S. dollars. Subscription fees and charges for single issues will be waived for organizations and individuals in countries where foreign-exchange regulations prohibit dollar payments.

Please address all correspondence, submissions, and orders to:

International Finance Section
Department of Economics, Fisher Hall
Princeton University
Princeton, New Jersey 08544-1021

List of Recent Publications

A complete list of publications may be obtained from the International Finance Section.

ESSAYS IN INTERNATIONAL FINANCE

152. G. K. Helleiner, *The IMF and Africa in the 1980s.* (July 1983)
153. Rachel McCulloch, *Unexpected Real Consequences of Floating Exchange Rates.* (August 1983)
154. Robert M. Dunn, Jr., *The Many Disappointments of Flexible Exchange Rates.* (December 1983)
155. Stephen Marris, *Managing the World Economy: Will We Ever Learn?* (October 1984)
156. Sebastian Edwards, *The Order of Liberalization of the External Sector in Developing Countries.* (December 1984)
157. Wilfred J. Ethier and Richard C. Marston, eds., with Kindleberger, Guttentag and Herring, Wallich, Henderson, and Hinshaw, *International Financial Markets and Capital Movements: A Symposium in Honor of Arthur I. Bloomfield.* (September 1985)
158. Charles E. Dumas, *The Effects of Government Deficits: A Comparative Analysis of Crowding Out.* (October 1985)
159. Jeffrey A. Frankel, *Six Possible Meanings of "Overvaluation": The 1981-85 Dollar.* (December 1985)
160. Stanley W. Black, *Learning from Adversity: Policy Responses to Two Oil Shocks.* (December 1985)
161. Alexis Rieffel, *The Role of the Paris Club in Managing Debt Problems.* (December 1985)
162. Stephen E. Haynes, Michael M. Hutchison, and Raymond F. Mikesell, *Japanese Financial Policies and the U.S. Trade Deficit.* (April 1986)
163. Arminio Fraga, *German Reparations and Brazilian Debt: A Comparative Study.* (July 1986)
164. Jack M. Guttentag and Richard J. Herring, *Disaster Myopia in International Banking.* (September 1986)
165. Rudiger Dornbusch, *Inflation, Exchange Rates, and Stabilization.* (October 1986)
166. John Spraos, *IMF Conditionality: Ineffectual, Inefficient, Mistargeted.* (December 1986)

167. Rainer Stefano Masera, *An Increasing Role for the ECU: A Character in Search of a Script.* (June 1987)
168. Paul Mosley, *Conditionality as Bargaining Process: Structural-Adjustment Lending, 1980-86.* (October 1987)
169. Paul Volcker, Ralph Bryant, Leonhard Gleske, Gottfried Haberler, Alexandre Lamfalussy, Shijuro Ogata, Jesús Silva-Herzog, Ross Starr, James Tobin, and Robert Triffin, *International Monetary Cooperation: Essays in Honor of Henry C. Wallich.* (December 1987)
170. Shafiqul Islam, *The Dollar and the Policy-Performance-Confidence Mix.* (July 1988)
171. James M. Boughton, *The Monetary Approach to Exchange Rates: What Now Remains?* (October 1988)
172. Jack M. Guttentag and Richard M. Herring, *Accounting for Losses On Sovereign Debt: Implications for New Lending.* (May 1989)
173. Benjamin J. Cohen, *Developing-Country Debt: A Middle Way.* (May 1989)
174. Jeffrey D. Sachs, *New Approaches to the Latin American Debt Crisis.* (July 1989)
175. C. David Finch, *The IMF: The Record and the Prospect.* (September 1989)
176. Graham Bird, *Loan-loss Provisions and Third-World Debt.* (November 1989)
177. Ronald Findlay, *The "Triangular Trade" and the Atlantic Economy of the Eighteenth Century: A Simple General-Equilibrium Model.* (March 1990)
178. Alberto Giovannini, *The Transition to European Monetary Union.* (November 1990)
179. Michael L. Mussa, *Exchange Rates in Theory and in Reality.* (December 1990)
180. Warren L. Coats, Jr., Reinhard W. Furstenberg, and Peter Isard, *The SDR System and the Issue of Resource Transfers.* (December 1990)
181. George S. Tavlas, *On the International Use of Currencies: The Case of the Deutsche Mark.* (March 1991)
182. Tommaso Padoa-Schioppa, ed., with Michael Emerson, Kumiharu Shigehara, and Richard Portes, *Europe after 1992: Three Essays.* (May 1991)
183. Michael Bruno, *High Inflation and the Nominal Anchors of an Open Economy.* (June 1991)

PRINCETON STUDIES IN INTERNATIONAL FINANCE

52. Irving B. Kravis and Robert E. Lipsey, *Toward an Explanation of National Price Levels.* (November 1983)
53. Avraham Ben-Basset, *Reserve-Currency Diversification and the Substitution Account.* (March 1984)
*54. Jeffrey Sachs, *Theoretical Issues in International Borrowing.* (July 1984)
55. Marsha R. Shelburn, *Rules for Regulating Intervention under a Managed Float.* (December 1984)
56. Paul De Grauwe, Marc Janssens and Hilde Leliaert, *Real-Exchange-Rate Variability from 1920 to 1926 and 1973 to 1982.* (September 1985)
57. Stephen S. Golub, *The Current-Account Balance and the Dollar: 1977-78 and 1983-84.* (October 1986)

58. John T. Cuddington, *Capital Flight: Estimates, Issues, and Explanations.* (December 1986)
59. Vincent P. Crawford, *International Lending, Long-Term Credit Relationships, and Dynamic Contract Theory.* (March 1987)
60. Thorvaldur Gylfason, *Credit Policy and Economic Activity in Developing Countries with IMF Stabilization Programs.* (August 1987)
61. Stephen A. Schuker, *American "Reparations" to Germany, 1919-33: Implications for the Third-World Debt Crisis.* (July 1988)
62. Steven B. Kamin, *Devaluation, External Balance, and Macroeconomic Performance: A Look at the Numbers.* (August 1988)
63. Jacob A. Frenkel and Assaf Razin, *Spending, Taxes, and Deficits: International-Intertemporal Approach.* (December 1988)
64. Jeffrey A. Frankel, *Obstacles to International Macroeconomic Policy Coordination.* (December 1988)
65. Peter Hooper and Catherine L. Mann, *The Emergence and Persistence of the U.S. External Imbalance, 1980-87.* (October 1989)
66. Helmut Reisen, *Public Debt, External Competitiveness, and Fiscal Discipline in Developing Countries.* (November 1989)
67. Victor Argy, Warwick McKibbin, and Eric Siegloff, *Exchange-Rate Regimes for a Small Economy in a Multi-Country World.* (December 1989)
68. Mark Gersovitz and Christina H. Paxson, *The Economies of Africa and the Prices of Their Exports.* (October 1990)
69. Felipe Larraín and Andrés Velasco, *Can Swaps Solve the Debt Crisis? Lessons from the Chilean Experience.* (November 1990)

SPECIAL PAPERS IN INTERNATIONAL ECONOMICS

15. Gene M. Grossman and J. David Richardson, *Strategic Trade Policy: A Survey of Issues and Early Analysis.* (April 1985)
16. Elhanan Helpman, *Monopolistic Competition in Trade Theory.* (June 1990)

REPRINTS IN INTERNATIONAL FINANCE

24. Peter B. Kenen, *Forward Rates, Interest Rates, and Expectations under Alternative Exchange Rate Regimes*; reprinted from *Economic Record* 61, 1985. (June 1986)
25. Jorge Braga de Macedo, *Trade and Financial Interdependence under Flexible Exchange Rates: The Pacific Area*; reprinted from *Pacific Growth and Financial Interdependence*, 1986. (June 1986)
26. Peter B. Kenen, *The Use of IMF Credit*; reprinted from *Pulling Together: The International Monetary Fund in a Multipolar World*, 1989. (December 1989)

The work of the International Finance Section is supported
in part by the income of the Walker Foundation, established
in memory of James Theodore Walker, Class of 1927. The
offices of the Section, in Fisher Hall, were provided by a
generous grant from Merrill Lynch & Company.

ISBN 0-88165-090-0